LOVERS POETRY

JAMES BUTLER

LOVERS
POETRY

JAMES BUTLER

TRAFFORD on demand publishing service ™

Order this book online at www.trafford.com
or email orders@trafford.com

Most Trafford titles are also available at major online book retailers.

Printed in the United States of America.

ISBN: 978-1-4269-4810-7 (sc)

Library of Congress Control Number: 2010918002

Trafford rev. 12/01/2010

Trafford
PUBLISHING®   www.trafford.com

North America & international
toll-free: 1 888 232 4444 (USA & Canada)
phone: 250 383 6864 ♦ fax: 812 355 4082

LOVERS POETRY is dedicated to:

My parents Maurice & Vivian,
my brothers, my sisters, my nieces,
my nephews, my granddaughters,
my son "Jaz", grandma Willie Belle,
Michele Eberlin, Michele Younkins,
Terri Dalpiaz-Mathers, Shelly Howell,
Cathy Hall, Lori Taylor, Sharon Taylor,
Velvet Wiggins, Mary Gallegher,
Nancy Kidd, Veronica Jackson,
Tiffany Pabian, Wilma Walton,Cindy Milner,
Mr. Louis Bator, Ed Jepson, John Ruiz,
Larry Braggs, Dru Huff, Steve Klos, Larry Sacco,
Randall "Randy" Chapman, Marcus "Dirty Red" Grice,
Donald Bennight for his help in preparing this manuscript,
Virginia Wilkinson, Kathy Kreis, David Keller,
Yvonne Bennage a.k.a. "Hennessy"
and to everyone whom loves poetic words of true love.

CONTENTS

HAVE YOU FOUND
SOMEONE TO LOVE

Is the condition of your heart
An experience you really treasure

Has there been a special someone
Reciting heartfelt words of love

Have you felt a tender kiss
That tore down a lonely wall

Do you catch yourself smiling
For no conscious reason at all

Does autumn sunrays upon your face
Remind you of someones caressments

Are you feeling like a flower
Sending forth its fragrant scent

Do you think life exceptionally lovely
Because love set your spirit free

Does wedding thoughts occupy your mind
Due to feeling so in love

Has someone convinced you totally
Staying together is meant to be

James Butler
11/20/2000

AWAKENED

I feel like a drawbridge
Has been lowered between us
Providing passage to one another

I will take my steps toward you
There is a halfway point to reach
You must take your steps toward me

The closer I approach how beautiful you are
Your bright eyes and luscious smile enchants
We can give birth to love and romance

Our inner chemistries create bliss and peace
Heart to heart we pair harmoniously
With our minds united our togetherness is victory

Your presence is felt without physical touch
I can taste your erotic craving in the air
Approach and yield to one another with lover care

Summon our souls become two as one surely
Vow vows to love one another purely
Step closer, step closer, draw nearer
Passage seems provided to one another

James Butler

GONDOLA ROMANCE

One needs spend leisure
On the canals of Venice

It ignites feelings of romance

Slowly paddled on liquid stillness
The sky aqua in hue

Silvery sunrays caressing golden tans
Soft hair brushed by fresh gentle breezes

Lingering embracements inciting feelings of belonging
Gondola passengers stirred with longing

The gift of smiles exchanged gleefully
Surprise trinkets given in gratuity

Poetry recited softly
Love an honored guest

Gondola drifting pass sidewalk cafes'
Lovers savoring a beautiful day

James Butler
11/26/2000

THE POETESS

A gentle June breeze
Coursed through her golden curls

Her skin of silken texture
Had celestial facial features

Summer morning blue eyes
Were set in cotton white

Long golden eye lashes
Caused the effect of sleep inducing fanning

Pouting shaped cherry lips smiled
Revealing even, milk white teeth

A voice the sound of holy angel harps
Lulled like a rock-a-by

She asked my name
Voluptuous breasts slowly heaved

Proud chin held dignified
Air of a virtuous queen

Love's radiance flowed from she
My heart felt stirred as well

She recited a poem of love
Said she created it just for me

Her recital produced the illusion
She is who I should marry

James Butler

WEDDING BELLS FOR ME

Who is going to marry me
For wedding bells to ring

Who will convince me of love
For wedding bells to sing

Who'll be true in heart for me
For wedding bells to chime

Who can be faithful in love
For wedding bells to herald

Who possesses the sheer goodness
For wedding bells consideration

Who is the worthy one
For wedding bells to greet us

Who is seeking happiness with a soul mate
For wedding bells to be assembled

Who will be right for oneness with me
For wedding bells to end aloneness

Who will exchange the words "I do"
For wedding bells to consummate love

James Butler

THE POETESS

A gentle June breeze
Coursed through her golden curls

Her skin of silken texture
Had celestial facial features

Summer morning blue eyes
Were set in cotton white

Long golden eye lashes
Caused the effect of sleep inducing fanning

Pouting shaped cherry lips smiled
Revealing even, milk white teeth

A voice the sound of holy angel harps
Lulled like a rock-a-by

She asked my name
Voluptuous breasts slowly heaved

Proud chin held dignified
Air of a virtuous queen

Love's radiance flowed from she
My heart felt stirred as well

She recited a poem of love
Said she created it just for me

Her recital produced the illusion
She is who I should marry

James Butler

WEDDING BELLS FOR ME

Who is going to marry me
For wedding bells to ring

Who will convince me of love
For wedding bells to sing

Who'll be true in heart for me
For wedding bells to chime

Who can be faithful in love
For wedding bells to herald

Who possesses the sheer goodness
For wedding bell's consideration

Who is the worthy one
For wedding bells to greet us

Who is seeking happiness with a soul mate
For wedding bells to be assembled

Who will be right for oneness with me
For wedding bells to end aloneness

Who will exchange the words "I do"
For wedding bells to consummate love

James Butler

A LOVER'S DESCRIPTION

Hair the color of golden sunrays
Skin the illumination of a cresent moon

Eyes the sea reflection of white clouds
And blue skies

Lips the slow drips of ripe sweet cherries
Not yet picked

Voice the sound of the wind savoringly
Caressing a late June meadow

Physique the awesome wonder of summertime
In full blossom

Personality the beauty and quietude
Of symphonic twilight

A lover the attainable essence
Of man's life

                              James Butler

CAN I KISS YOU

    Can I kiss you
Do say yes, please
We share   mutual attraction
Love is mirrored in our eyes

Your lips are luscious
Your lips look warm
Your lips look soft
Let your lips not be witheld

I will kiss so sweetly
I will be so gentle
My lips are warm
my lips are soft

I crave kissing you
Our lips need only touch
Five seconds would seem an hour
Lips to lips would be so savored

                              James Butler

.THE SOFT KISS

Your lips came to mine
Liken to an autumn breeze
As though to be the last
A kiss you felt we needed

Textures barely tangible
Sensations of light caressments
Warmth a consuming current
Our minds spiraled torrently

Every carnal sense were afire
We dreaded such bliss to end
Our hearts played harmonious cords of love
I cared to kiss unending

James Butler

DAWN LOVEMAKING
IN DECEMBER

Snow softly falling
It earth's blanket everywhere

Chimney smoke rising
Sunlight peeping along east's horizon

Bare elms creeking in a mild wind
Ponds are frozen with ice still thin

Bedroom fireplace crackling of hickory
Two stir awake on a bear rug warmly

Cuddled embracingly, kissing slowly
Whispered endearments setting hearts aglow

Four hips sleepily in passionate throe
Love and desire the occasion's toll

Last moans greeted by a risen sun
Pleasure and contentment once again fun

James Butler
11/21/2000

TWILIGHT TENDERNESS

Drawn snugly together
Impassioned with love

Bodies desires aflamed
Lips kissing tamed

Carnal tastes sweet
Chest caressing breasts

Navel to navel
Groans following moans

Warm thighs entwined
Stars twinkling bright

Arms embracing gently
Thrill preceding spills

James Butler
11/28/2000

ENTOURAGE OF A
LOVER'S SILHOUETTE

Upon a balconey
Posed at night
Moon shining bright

Gentle breeze aflow
Silk gown aglow

Petite desirous body
Tiny bare feet

Tapered thighs trailing
Pubic perfume availing

Smooth curvy hips
Flat belly churning

Small upturned palms
Slim fingers beckoning me

Pink gown see-through
Breast nipples succulent

Neck slender taffy
Head held high

Pretty face illuminated
Soul searching eyes

Waist length hair
Silky blonde strands

A beauty silhouetted
Entire presence felt

James Butler

YOU TOUCHED ME

You touched me
Befriending me during need

You touched me
Helping through troubled times

You touched me
Sacrificing that you could not

You touched me
Giving of self generously

You touched me
Speaking my name sweetly

You touched me
With love- filled eyes

You touched me
Holding my hands gently

You touched me
Through your warm embrace

You touched me
Kissing my lips tenderly

You touched me
Assuring me of your love

You touched me
Vowing you are mine

You touched me
I am sincerely yours

James Butler
11/28/2000

SPECIAL DANCE

I want to dance with you
It could be on a cresent moon
Or on the colorful ring of Saturn
Dancing slowly so close

Whispering cherished endearments
You to me and I to you
Dancing on no gravity
Leaving footprints on Venus and Mars

The excited beats of our hearts
Heard in the quiet of the universe
Twinkling stars as candlelights
The Milky Way a danceroom floor

I want to dance with you
With you it is my dream
It can be eternally
Dance on the oceantop
Peaks of mountains too
Earth a renewed paradise for you and me

Happiness and peace shared comfortingly
In one anothers arms
Step by step, one, two, three
Love the enchanting music we hear playing

James Butler

SIMPLE ENDEARMENTS

I am never speechless having
Words of sincere love for you

You are all I ever hoped for
Your existence fulfills my dreams

Your friendship is enemy to loneliness
I never feel lonely

When sick or feeling blue
You are a healer and joy giver

Goodness consistently reeks from you
I hold your interests at heart

Your life is of high value to me
Noone has comparision sea to sea

Your caresses are like warm sunrays
I am drunken by your kiss

Nature is illuminated by your presence
You make my life worth living

I cherish your love given freely
You makes my life complete

James Butler
11/28/2000

MY SOLITAIRE

Gem of gems is my beloved
Set alone with no comparision

Most beautiful of all on earth
More costly than the whole universe

Jewel of soft fleshly warmth
Embracements rich security

Kisses of royalty enthroned on mine
Keeper of my love ordained by HE divine

A friend above friends
Love that never forsakes

Forever dearly cherished
Happiness of my life

James Butler

FANTASIES OF YOU

I have had fantasies of you
Coming to me in the night
I sat at our gazebo
Many stars shone brightly

Crickets played a September symphony
Nightingales sung of a love we share
Fireflies alerted me to your approach
Your silhouette was hypnotic in moonbeams

Gentle breezes rippled satin against your curves
Dew sacredly purified your running bare feet
I stood up and extended my arms toward you
It seemed eternity before you reached my embrace

I know a man's woe of not having a mate
It is not seeing eyes revealing love as yours do
It is the absence of a voice as yours whispering songful
It is not knowing kisses of commitment as yours give

James Butler

HERE I AM

Here I am
All yours to see
All yours to know
All yours to love

All yours to claim
I am receptive
I am in love
You are my choice

Be all mine to see
All mine to know
All mine to love
Care to be claimed

Chance love with me
Do be receptive
Happiness can be ours
Can I be your choice

James Butler

OUR SHARED TEARS

Cheek to cheek
Soft fleshly warmth
Sheened by tears
Such pouring flow

Our hearts messengers
Unadulterated liquid truths
Proclaiming our love
Exclaiming sheer joy

Streams of emotion
Strengthening our union
Freeing our souls
Sealing dear kisses

Ascending from purity
Descending to nudity
Existing to impassion
Drops of peace

James Butler

MY LOVER'S SMILE

Vibrant with robust
Disarming all distrust
Warmly befriending
Loving messenger of God

Terrestial-celestial beauty
Rose petals tenderness
Golden sunrays magnificence
Silvery moonbeams brilliance

Cheerful portrait of love
Beauteous spacious sky
Symphonic constellation
Soft song of summertime

Gentle soothing breeze
Mediterranean sunrise
Sight of joyous life
Poetic smile of smiles

James Butler

GENTLE TOUCH

Lovers what is gentle touch to you
I will describe what it is to me

Cirrus clouds on a mid-summer day
Quietly adrift against a soft blue sky

Roses, tulips and lilacs freshly bloomed
Their flowery scents created as nature's perfume

Bright green grass neatly mown
Many acres of it appearing to be a still sea

Magnolia tree boasting colorful floret displays
With silvery green leaves producing shade

The busy wings of a hummingbird
Its long beak drinking nectar free

Caressing breezes blowing my eyes lashes
Gracefully fanning my head

Sweet blackberries along a hilly deer trail
Choice with thick dumplings for making a cobbler

A cool lake with shadowed lily pads
As the sun yawningly smiles on the western horizon
To end another day

James Butler

www.ingramcontent.com/pod-product-compliance
Lightning Source LLC
Chambersburg PA
CBHW072039060426
42449CB00010BA/2349